Introduction

I want to thank you and congratulate you for downloading the book, "Berries! An Introduction To Growing Organic Backyard Berries".

This book contains proven steps and strategies on how to grow berries right in your own backyard. Berries are very sweet and delectable, perfect as snacks, desserts, or part of salads and other dishes. With buying them commercially, you run the risk of buying berries that are laden with chemicals from fertilizers, pesticides and such. All the goodness can get ruined by these harmful chemicals.

The good thing is, you can grow your own berries and make sure that they are fully organic. You can control what goes into the plant and eventually into the fruits. The sweetest berries are ones that come from your own care and hard work.

Read this book and find out how. In no time, you will be enjoying the "fruits" of your labor.

Thanks again for downloading this book, I hope you enjoy it!

- Jamie

A Brief Introduction to Berries & Organic Farming

Berries are sweet, juicy and luscious fruits that captivate the palates of so many people. You can enjoy them fresh or frozen. You can eat them as is or turn them into something else. You can add berries to your salads; you can also use them as topping for sundaes, cakes, pancakes and several other foods, and you can also bake berries into bread and pastries. You can cook berries in sugar, can them, and turn them into delicious jams and preserves. They are delectable in many ways.

The most delicious way to enjoy berries is to enjoy them fresh and organic. Even more so if they are grown right in your own backyard, raised with your own two hands.

Organic Farming

Organic farming simply means not using synthetic chemicals on plants. This includes not using any herbicides for weed control, pesticides and insecticides for pest control and synthetic fertilizers for enhanced growth and fruiting,

This type of farming means using natural ways to promote growth and make them bear fruit. It also means using natural methods of getting rid of pests. This includes the use of nets to protect the plants from insects, birds and small mammals (rodents, raccoons, squirrels, etc.).

To discourage the growth of weeds, you must not use herbicides. You need to pull them out by hand and apply mulch on the surface of the soil to prevent them from growing again. In fact, organic farming heavily relies on mulch for weed control. Not only that, mulch is also a source of natural fertilizer. Other ways to improve growth and fertility is by applying natural sources of ammonia such as dried kelp and fish.

Organically grown berries are the best in terms of taste, quality and safety. Chemicals from pesticides and fertilizers leave harmful residues on the fruits, which stay on the fruits even after washing. Sometimes, these chemicals incorporate themselves into the very flesh of the berry, and this can adversely affect their flavor and nutritional value. The best way to make sure that the berries you and your family consume are 100% organic is to plant them yourself in your own backyard.

Backyard Blueberries

Blueberries are both delicious and packed with nutrients. Nutrition experts consider them as superfruits because they contain an abundance of phytonutrients, antioxidants, minerals and vitamins. They are also super delicious. You can eat them fresh off the bushes, cooked in sugar, made into jams, preserved or baked into pies, breads, and cakes.

Planting

The best time to plant blueberries is during the latter portion of the winter season; you can also start in the early days of spring, within 6 weeks before the last spring frost. However, if you sprout seedlings in containers indoors, you can transplant them into the ground later; just make sure that there is ample time for the roots to grow before the summer season starts.

The planting site should receive a good amount of sun. The soil should have good drainage and with an acidic pH, preferably pH 4 to 5.5. The soil should also be well aerated, very high in humus and moist. Young plants need soil with an abundance of organic matter in the shallow layers. You can add leaf compost or rotting sawdust to the soil if there is not enough organic matter. Prepare the soil in the fall. This will allow ample time for the added organic matter to settle. This way, the young blueberry seedlings will have a better chance of survival.

If the soil pH is at 5.5 to 6.0, improve the acidity with a top dressing of soil sulfur. Do this two times in a year to maintain the ideal pH.

If the soil pH is lacking in acidity, here is what you should do:

- Dig a hole 2 feet deep and 6 feet wide to plant the blueberries.

- Fill the hole with a mixture of equal parts sand and peat moss.

- Allow the organic material to settle.

- Mulch the bed using aged sawdust. This material is acidic. Other organic materials may also be used.

- Fertilize the soil annually using balanced organic fertilizer.

- Watering and irrigation should be acidic. If using hard water, add two teaspoons of vinegar for every gallon of water to acidify it before using on the plant.

If the soil pH is more than 6.0, it is better to grow the blueberries in large containers filled with bark-based or wood chip-based planting mixture.

You should also consider the spacing between the blueberry bushes before you start planting. For the lowbush varieties, there should be 12 inches of space in between plants. For saskatoons, space them 1 to 2 feet apart. For highbush plants, space them 4 feet apart. For rabbiteyes, plant them 6 feet apart.

Planting depth should be the same as the depth as in the containers while they started out. Water the plants well and add mulch to the surface of the soil. Add acidic mulch, about 2 inches thick. Prune all shoots except for the two most upright and most vigorously growing ones.

After planting, water the plants well. For the next few weeks, give about 2 inches of water or roughly ½ to 1 gallon of water per square foot. Water the root zone every week.

Mulching

Mulching is very important to promote good growth and fertility. As the organic materials decompose over time, they slowly release nutrients that fertilize the plant. The best materials to use for mulch include pine needles, maple leaves, and oak leaves. Shred these before spreading over the soil. Pine bark may also be used. It lasts for about 2 to 3 seasons.

Dress mulch once there are bare areas showing. Weeds would quickly grow through these patches so you need to cover them up as soon as you can. For blueberries, the mulch should be 3 inches or more in thickness, and coarsely shredded to allow water to penetrate easily while still discouraging the growth of weeds. If you do not shred the leaves before applying them around the base of the stem, they could deflect water and prevent the roots from absorbing enough to supply the plant's needs.

Never use mulch that has been treated with synthetic chemicals, preservatives, pesticides, and such. Also, never use organic material that came from plants that were infected with pests or diseases. All these can bring trouble to the plant.

Fertilizing

Fertilizing promotes better growth and more fruits. However, you need to use fertilizer in the right amounts, of the right type, and at the right time. Adding too much fertilizer during the growing season will only result in more branches. The plant will look messy, and harvesting will be difficult because of the thick foliage. More branches also mean that the plant will be bearing fewer fruits.

Put on a top dress of organic fertilizer anytime between the early to the middle part of spring. The amount depends on how old the plant is. For 3 to 5-year old plants, sprinkle ½ to 1 pound of organic fertilizer. For plants older than five years, top dress with 1 pound or about 3 cups of organic fertilizer. Sprinkle the fertilizer over the growing zone.

In late May to the early days of June, repeat the top dressing. This time, use only half of the amount you used during the early spring days. This will encourage more flowers to bloom and bear larger berries the following year. This second top dressing is only necessary if you will not be using liquid fertilizer.

Start giving the plants a liquid feeding once the blooms have fallen, which is probably near the start of August. Give it every two weeks. Apply the liquid fertilizer to the foliage once the plant starts to flower and until green berries appear. Apply the liquid fertilizer to the root zone via hose or drip line during the fruiting period. Apply another round of feeding after harvesting.

For the liquid fertilizer, use this recipe:

·   In a gallon of clean water, add half a tablespoon of blackstrap molasses, half tablespoon of liquid kelp such as Maxicrop, and 2 tablespoons of fish fertilizer such as Neptune's Harvest (2-4-1) Fish Fertilizer.

When providing liquid feedings, you need to saturate the entire plant. The leaves (if applying to the foliage) and the ground over the root zone must be soaking wet. Avoid over watering, though. Too much fertilizer can drown the roots and might even burn the plant. Irrigate the plants a day before liquid feeding or wait until after a rain shower (if one is likely within the feeding schedule). Mature plants should receive about 5 gallons of liquid fertilizer per dose, less for younger plants.

Many other fertilizers can used, such as those sprayed on the foliage. However, avoid spraying if the mature plants are already fruiting and near harvest. Doing so will give the berries a fishy taste.

Give foliar treatments post-harvest. This helps to increase the next year's yield. It also increases the plant's vigor, after having spent its nutrients and energy into bearing fruits.

Pruning

Prune any broken or dead branches at the start of spring. Look for long, thin branches that are growing horizontally near the plant's base. These growths do not do much for the plant, except to mooch off the plant's energy and reduce productivity.

It is also important to keep the blueberry bush open. Sunlight should enter deep into the bush. Remove all twiggy branches as these will not be bearing any large, good fruits anyway. Removing twigs may reduce yield a little but the berries will be larger and have better quality. This will also encourage new vertical growth, which is better for the plant.

Flowering and Fruiting

When flowers emerge in the first year after planting, pick them off. This will give better pay off in the years to come. This will make the plants concentrate their energy into growing stronger and more vigorous instead of bearing fruit. During dry spells, water them well. Add mulch whenever necessary and make sure that it is always 2-inches deep. Apply organic fertilizer lightly during the spring. In late summer, apply more fertilizer to encourage the growth of more flower buds.

Once the fruits start to emerge, so would the birds, bugs, and other small animals. A good net over the plant should be enough to keep the developing fruits safe from these unwelcome invaders. Start harvesting fruits once they turn blue. Do this twice a week.

It may take a few years before your plants can yield a substantial harvest, but the wait will be well worth it.

Backyard Blackberries

Blackberries in the making

Most people do not consider blackberries when planning for a backyard berry garden, mostly because blackberries already grow well in the wild. However, if you grow them in your backyard, you get to improve their size and quality. Tamed blackberries produce fruits that are larger, sweeter and juicier compared to their wild counterparts. They also retain their delectable flavors very well even after freezing.

There are two basic types of blackberry plants - erect and trailing. Erect plants grow from arched canes. The canes can support themselves in an upright growing condition without the additional support from trellises. Trailing varieties, however, cannot support the plant for an upright growth. They need to grow around trellises. Fruits from erect plants also ripen later and are smaller and less sweet compared to those born from the trailing variety.

Choose the cultivar suited to your area. Blackberry plants may be tough, but extreme temperature changes can still harm them.

Soil and Planting Site

Blackberries grow well in just about any type of soil. Experts have observed that the plants grow best and produce better yields when in moderately light, loamy soil types. Adding humus to this type of soil further improves the growing conditions. The soil pH is ideally slightly acidic, around pH 6.0.

Blackberries need full sun exposure in order to grow. The length and amount of sun exposure determine how much fruit they will yield; more sun means more fruits. If the plant gets even a slight amount of shade, the berries develop a tart flavor.

The planting site should have good drainage. That is, the water drains within a few hours after watering. If not, then plant on raised mounds or in large containers.

Water is crucial for the growth and development of blackberry bushes. You need to give the plants lots of water during the fruiting season and decrease the amount during the winter as it may cause frost damage.

If you intend to train the blackberries to grow on trellises, set a 6-feet distance in between the plants. When planting erect blackberry varieties, they should have ample space (about 2 feet) in between them. There should be 10 feet of distance between the rows. These spaces would allow room for maneuvering when working with the plants. It also prevents the branches from tangling as they grow. If planting blackberries next to other types of berries, be mindful that not all berries work well together. For instance, do not plant the Black Walnut blackberry variety close to blueberries because this variety is toxic to blueberry plants.

Plant your blackberries in the early spring when in the Northern regions, or late winter to early spring when in the South. Soak the roots in water before transplanting them into the ground, especially if they look dry. To plant, shove a large fork or shovel into the ground and rock it back and forth. Widen the slit just enough to accommodate the roots without breaking or cramping them. Trim the tops off the plant and leave around 6 inches, before putting them into the ground. Plant them at the same depth they were when they started out.

Avoid soil compaction around the roots. Allow the soil any media to settle around the roots naturally. During the entire growing season, constantly soak the soil around the root zone.

Mulching

Mulch the plants with straw immediately after planting. Pile it up to about 4 to 6 inches deep. Keep it thick through the plants' first winter because roots are still establishing themselves and are very susceptible to damage.

How the blackberries will develop depends on the amount of mulch. Juiciness requires a lot of water during the entire fruiting season. Keep the mulch thick especially throughout this time. Ample amounts of water will also help the plant to bear more fruits.

If you do not have any hay for mulch, you can use black, biodegradable plastic bags to cover the root zone of your blackberries; garbage bags work well in this case. It will protect against loss of moisture by effectively trapping the moisture within the root zone. Cover the base of the plant in black plastic then cover the plastic with other organic mulch such as bark and pine needles. Exposing the plastic to sunlight speeds up its degradation, allowing weeds to poke through and eventually overrun the rows. Keep a good water supply underneath the plastic. A drip irrigation system can supply adequate moisture under the black plastic.

Pine needles are also good mulching material. The needles naturally form a stable layout, which means more stable mulch. Pine needles are also lightweight, which reduces the probability of the mulch compaction and smothering the plant. It also helps that pine needle mulch lasts longer compared to other types. When using this material for mulch, spread them evenly over the root zone. Pile them up to 4 inches. The consistent soil moisture underneath the needles would help promote better quality and higher production.

Pine bark is also good mulch material for blackberry plants. It is readily available in most gardening stores, as nuggets or already shredded. The nugget form lasts longer than the shredded ones. However, they are very vulnerable to soil erosion. A good downpour is enough to wash away a huge chunk of the mulch. Shredded bark pieces are smaller than the nuggets but hold their place even after a rainstorm.

Wheat straw is another good organic mulching material. It also provides good insulation, which is perfect during the long winter months, while retaining a good amount of moisture in the roots. It is also cheaper. The downside to using wheat straw is that when it decomposes, it leaches nitrogen away from the soil. Nitrogen is very important for blackberries. This compound is important for photosynthesis and chlorophyll production. Straw can also harbor the seeds of weeds. It is also a very flammable material, putting the plants at risk for fires especially during dry spells.

Training and Pruning

Training blackberries would apply more to the trailing varieties, and it is fairly easy to do. Simply tie the healthy, vigorously growing canes to a fence or a trellis.

New canes and suckers emerge and if you leave them untended, and they will cause the plant to become a tangled mess. It can easily grow into a thicket that does not bear much fruit.

Get into pruning the plants early as new canes tend to grow quickly and they may overwhelm you. When left unmanaged, there will too many unproductive canes and mowing the entire row and starting over would be much better. To avoid this, get to pruning early on.

Canes that produced fruits in the last year will no longer bear any fruits the following season, so start pruning these branches as soon as you harvest from them. Do this in the late days of August and into September. Aside from these, take out all new canes that look sickly or thin. Leave about four of the sturdiest and vigorous new canes.

Tie the new blackberry canes together. These would be the ones expected to bear fruits in the next year. Apply mulch again using straw. Pile them to about 6-8 inches thick.

Backyard Raspberries

Another favorite is raspberries. Blackberries and raspberries are often mistaken for each other because of the close resemblance. The main method of differentiating them is the appearance of the harvested fruit. Raspberries have a hollow center once harvested because he core remains attached to the stem. The fruit comes in several colors. The most popular have reddish hues, but they also come in yellow, purple and black. The red ones have a fruity, tangy flavor, and the plant tends to produce more fruits than the other colors. Reds and yellows are also among the hardiest. Blacks are the weakest and most vulnerable to diseases.

These plants thrive in zones between 3 and 9 (for more about hardiness zones follow this link http://planthardiness.ars.usda.gov/PHZMWeb/) Different cultivars are available to suit specific climates. There are extra-hardy cultivars suited for the cold climates of the Northern areas. There are also some heat-tolerant varieties that are suitable for the South.

Good air circulation is important because of the risk for diseases. However, avoid sites where there are high winds that will whip the raspberry canes around and possibly damage them. When planted, the raspberries should be at least 30 meters or 1,000 feet away from wild blackberries and other brambleberries to prevent the risk of cross-pollination.

Types

Raspberry varieties are classified as ever-bearing, summer-bearing, and fall-bearing. Summer-bearers have their major fruit production throughout the summer, fall-bearers in the fall. Ever-bearers produce fruits twice a year - during the early days of summer and during the fall. There is also the newer "Heritage" variety. It bears moderate amounts of large red raspberries during the summer, on the old canes of the plant, and during the fall season, it bears a much heavier crop on the new canes.

Planting

The best time to plant raspberries is during the fall. The soil should be prepared by enriching it with organic compost, well-rotted manure or leaf mold. The soil should be thoroughly cultivated for a few months after planting the rootstock.

You need to plant the raspberries on mounds or ridges, especially if the soil tends to get seasonally wet. Create rows about 18 to 24 inches. Create a gradual rise towards the middle of the mound. The grade height should be about 6 to 8 inches. Ridge planting helps the plant to produce almost twice the yield during the wet years.

Planting in ridges benefits most varieties of raspberries, but not all of them. This includes the Lauren red raspberry, which produces more berries with better qualities. Anne Golden fall raspberry, purple and black raspberries, however, do not thrive better in the ridge method. For cultivars that don't thrive well in ridges, choose a site with good drainage or you can plant them in raised beds or large containers.

Fertilizing

Raspberries often do not need much care and attention, but a little extra attention increases crop yields. Follow a care schedule to get a larger quantity and larger raspberries.

Top-dress the plants during the late days of April. Place one-fourth of a pound of fertilizer for every 1-foot row. If the raspberries are in mounds, place a top-dress of half a pound for every 3-inch (diameter) mound.

Apply another batch of organic fertilizer when the plants are about to set forth blooms. Apply only half of the amount placed in April.

Once the new canes of fall-bearing raspberries emerge and grow out, start a liquid feeding schedule. For summer raspberries, liquid feeding starts when canes sprout and start flowering. Check the berries regularly. Two weeks before they are about to ripen, stop liquid feedings to the foliage to avoid a fishy-tasting fruit.

Do your liquid feedings when the temperatures during the day are consistently not more than 60 degrees. This will increase the plant's vigor and help it bear more fruits. It also improves the plant's resistance to disease and pests.

Mulching

Mulching is often discouraged with raspberries, but it can really be helpful if the right kind is used. Mulch should be coarse, easily dries out, and does not form mats. Some good mulching material would be straw or pine nuggets. Avoid using grass clippings, hay, unshredded leaves, wood chips and mulch from hardwood bark. The worst mulch is grass because it can trigger a bad weed problem.

Before mulching, place granular fertilizers. Replace the mulch when bare patches start to show.

Watering

During the dry seasons, establish an irrigation line. Soak the rows with about 2 gallons of water for every 1 foot along the row. When applied using drip lines, the rate should be ½ gallon per hour. Do this two times a week.

Pruning

Pruning is important in order to encourage higher and better yields. Removing branches helps the plant to concentrate its energies on fruit development.

Suckers would grow off the main plant, near the base. Regularly prune these but leave 6-8 new canes. Retain those that are growing about 1 inch from the level of the soil. These are still necessary for the plant to achieve proper development. These canes should not grow more than 30 inches high. The best time to remove canes is after the harvesting season.

To encourage better crops during the fall in ever-bearers, cut off any of the old canes growing at ground level. Do this after they have already borne fruit. Red, summer-bearing raspberries bear fruits on canes that are two years old. After this time, cut them off. For purple and black raspberries, the fruits are borne on the side branches growing off the older canes. Cut these off after a harvest in the summer. For new canes that are 3-4 feet long, clip the tips off. This will encourage them to grow branches. For all varieties, remove all the branches that look old and are grayish-brown in color. During the late days of winter, chop off all small canes but leave about 3 to 6 of the sturdier ones for every 1 foot along the planted rows. Remove any of the spindly branches growing on the sides. For all other side branches, trim them back to 20-25 centimeters or 8-10 inches long.